Sora by OpenAI

Is It a Game-Changer for Artificial Intelligence?

An Expert Guide to Its Capabilities,

Limitations, and the Future of Video

Creation

Joe E. Grayson

Table of Contents

Introduction

Artificial intelligence has become one of the most transformative forces of the 21st century, redefining industries and reshaping the way we interact with technology. From machine learning algorithms that recommend what to watch next to autonomous vehicles navigating city streets, AI has evolved at an extraordinary pace. Its capabilities have extended far beyond simple automation, now venturing into realms of creativity, innovation, and decision-making that were once thought to be exclusively human domains. This rapid evolution has not only changed how businesses operate but has also begun to influence the very fabric of society, from education and healthcare to entertainment and communication.

In the realm of modern communication, video has emerged as the dominant medium. Whether for education, storytelling, marketing, or social interaction, video content drives engagement and captures attention in ways that text or static images often cannot. As this demand grows, so too does the need for tools that can meet the ever-increasing appetite for dynamic, high-quality video production. Traditional video creation, however, is labor-intensive, requiring significant time, skill, and resources. This is where artificial intelligence has stepped in, offering new possibilities that are both exciting and, at times, unsettling.

Among the most remarkable advancements in this field is the development of tools like Sora by OpenAI. Sora represents a new frontier in video creation, leveraging AI to generate videos from simple text prompts. It is not just another editing tool or animation software; it is a breakthrough that reimagines the entire process of video production. By translating words into moving visuals, Sora has opened up opportunities for creators, educators, and marketers to produce compelling video content faster and more efficiently than ever before. It combines innovation with accessibility, making advanced video generation technology available to users of all skill levels.

This book takes an in-depth look at Sora, exploring its capabilities, limitations, and potential to revolutionize video creation. By delving into how this tool works, what it can achieve, and where it struggles, the journey through these pages aims to provide a comprehensive understanding of what makes Sora a pivotal milestone in AI innovation. Moreover, it will examine the broader implications of AI-driven video creation for industries, creators, and society as a whole. Through a detailed and nuanced exploration, the narrative will highlight how tools like Sora are shaping the future of communication and creativity, offering a glimpse into a world where the boundaries of imagination and technology converge seamlessly.

Chapter 1: Understanding AI-Generated Video

The concept of AI video generation embodies the remarkable ability of machines to create moving visuals from textual descriptions, data inputs, or pre-existing images. At its core, this technology leverages algorithms and deep learning models to analyze, interpret, and reconstruct video frames in a coherent sequence, offering outputs that were once the domain of skilled human creators. What distinguishes AI video generation from traditional methods is its efficiency, adaptability, and creative potential. It can craft narratives, replicate complex animations, or produce lifelike scenes, all by interpreting a few user prompts or inputs.

To appreciate how we arrived at this juncture, it is essential to trace the historical journey of AI's evolution in visual media. The initial forays of artificial intelligence into visual creativity were through static images. AI tools like GANs (Generative Adversarial Networks) showcased their ability to create realistic images by training on massive datasets. Early applications focused on refining image resolution, restoring old photographs, or even generating entirely new artworks that mirrored human creativity.

These milestones laid the groundwork for the leap to video generation. Creating videos, however, introduced a higher level of complexity. Unlike static images, videos require temporal consistency, realistic movement, and adherence to physical dynamics to maintain believability. Achieving this demanded advancements in computational power, neural network architecture, and the ability to model not just pixels but the passage of time.

As AI evolved, breakthroughs in motion synthesis and image-to-video transformation became stepping stones. AI began not only to recognize objects within images but also to predict their movement and behavior over time. Experiments with AI-driven animation, such as style transfer onto video frames, marked the transition from static to dynamic. Tools initially focused on adding motion to still images, creating looping videos or simple animations. Over time, these systems grew more sophisticated, capable of generating short clips with layered actions and photorealistic details.

Today, AI video generation represents the convergence of years of innovation in machine learning, computer vision, and creative AI systems. Tools like Sora harness these developments to create video content that not only interprets textual instructions but also incorporates intricate visual details, mimicking artistic styles or real-world physics. This progression from generating single images to complex video sequences illustrates the boundless potential of AI, where the distinction between human-crafted and machine-created visuals continues to blur.

The distinction between static AI imagery tools like DALL·E and dynamic AI video generation tools lies primarily in the complexity of their outputs and the challenges involved in producing them. While both leverage advanced machine learning algorithms to interpret inputs and create visual content, the shift from generating single images to continuous video sequences introduces unique technical and conceptual hurdles.

Static AI imagery tools, such as DALL·E, are designed to produce a single frame or image based on a textual description. Their focus is on crafting visually accurate and contextually relevant scenes within a confined space and time. The generated output exists as a standalone piece, requiring no concern for movement, temporal coherence, or evolving elements. These systems excel at understanding spatial relationships, texture, lighting, and artistic styles within the boundaries of one image, allowing for impressive creativity and realism in their outputs.

Dynamic AI video tools, on the other hand, operate on a completely different plane of complexity. Videos are not isolated snapshots but sequences of frames that must flow seamlessly to create the illusion of movement and progression over time. This requires the AI to maintain consistency across frames while respecting real-world physics, object permanence, and temporal logic. For example, if an object moves from one side of the screen to another, the AI must ensure it remains coherent in size, shape, and trajectory across all intermediate frames—a challenge far beyond static image generation.

Another critical difference lies in the aspect of storytelling. While an image captures a single moment, a video must convey a sequence of events, emotions, or actions, requiring a deeper understanding of narrative structure and context. This means dynamic video tools must interpret not just what the user wants to see but also how elements within the scene interact, evolve, and react to one another over time.

Additionally, the computational demands for video generation far exceed those of image creation. A single high-resolution image may require considerable processing power, but generating dozens of similar-quality frames per second for a video multiplies this demand exponentially. Dynamic tools must also tackle challenges like frame blending, motion interpolation, and ensuring realism in areas such as shadows, reflections, and object interactions.

In essence, while static AI imagery tools focus on creating one stunning moment, dynamic video tools aim to bring those moments to life by adding the dimensions of time and movement. This evolution from still to motion not only broadens the scope of AI applications but also raises the bar for technological innovation and creative potential.

Chapter 2: Sora's Debut

OpenAI's development of Sora reflects a continuous journey of innovation aimed at pushing the boundaries of AI in creative applications. Known for breakthroughs like GPT for text generation and DALL-E for static image creation, OpenAI's foray into video generation was a natural progression. The goal was to develop a tool that could interpret textual inputs and transform them into dynamic, coherent video outputs, opening up possibilities for creators, educators, and businesses to produce engaging content with unprecedented ease.

The earlier version of Sora, introduced nine months ago, marked its initial steps into the public eye. However, at that stage, access to the tool was tightly controlled, and its use was limited to selected demonstrations curated by

OpenAI. These demonstrations showcased carefully designed prompts, highlighting Sora's potential while minimizing exposure to its limitations. The tool's capacity to interpret complex inputs and generate visually compelling results made a strong impression, but its true capabilities remained shrouded in exclusivity.

During this phase, Sora served primarily as a proof of concept, with OpenAI leveraging the feedback and results from these controlled scenarios to refine its algorithms. The system was a marvel of technical innovation, but it also faced significant challenges. Realistic motion, object permanence, and consistency across frames posed hurdles that required iterative improvements. OpenAI's selective approach allowed them to test the waters, gauge public reception, and further optimize the tool before considering broader accessibility.

This limited-access phase provided valuable insights into both the promise and the pitfalls of AI video generation. It also hinted at the transformative potential of a tool like Sora once it reached a more mature stage. By laying this foundation, OpenAI set the stage for Sora's transition from a fascinating experimental project to a robust and accessible platform poised to revolutionize video creation.

The transition of Sora from a limited-access experimental tool to one available for public use marks a pivotal moment in the evolution of AI-driven video generation. By opening its capabilities to creators worldwide, OpenAI has shifted Sora from being a proof-of-concept innovation to a practical tool that democratizes video production. This move signifies a broader vision to make advanced technology accessible to a diverse audience, empowering individuals and organizations with a powerful new medium for storytelling and communication.

For creators, the public access rollout of Sora represents an unprecedented opportunity to transform how video content is conceived and produced. Traditional video creation often demands a significant investment of time, technical expertise, and resources. From scripting and shooting to editing and rendering, the process can be daunting, particularly for smaller teams or individuals without access to professional tools. Sora eliminates many of these barriers by enabling users to generate videos from simple text prompts, dramatically reducing the time and effort required to bring ideas to life.

This accessibility is a game-changer for content creators, educators, marketers, and businesses. With Sora, creators can experiment with diverse visual styles, generate animations, or produce abstract designs without needing advanced skills in video editing or animation. It offers a level playing field where creativity, rather than technical prowess, becomes the key driver of content production. Whether it's a solo entrepreneur crafting marketing campaigns or a teacher developing educational materials, Sora opens doors to new possibilities.

However, this transition also introduces challenges and responsibilities. The widespread availability of a tool as powerful as Sora raises questions about authenticity, ethical use, and the potential for misuse. For instance, the ability to produce hyper-realistic or persuasive videos at scale could be exploited to spread misinformation or deceive audiences. OpenAI has implemented safeguards, such as content restrictions and watermarks, to address these concerns, but the implications of mass access to such technology warrant careful consideration.

For creators, the shift to public access means navigating a new landscape where AI-generated videos become a standard part of the creative toolkit. It challenges them to explore new ways of storytelling, push creative boundaries, and adapt to a world where the distinction between human-made and machine-generated visuals continues to blur. The public release of Sora is not just about convenience—it's about reimagining the possibilities of video creation and redefining the relationship between imagination and technology.

Chapter 3: The User Experience

The Sora interface has been thoughtfully designed to provide a balance between functionality and simplicity, catering to both seasoned creators and novices exploring video generation for the first time. Its intuitive layout makes navigating the tool seamless, allowing users to focus on crafting their ideas rather than wrestling with complicated settings. By structuring its features in a user-friendly manner, Sora empowers users to experiment with creativity while maintaining control over the results.

The interface is divided into key sections, each serving a specific purpose. On the left-hand side, users can explore a repository of inspiration, including prompts generated by other users. This feature not only showcases the diversity of Sora's capabilities but also provides a learning opportunity by displaying the exact prompts used to achieve specific results. For those looking to customize or tweak existing content, the interface offers a remix feature, where users can modify these prompts to produce tailored versions of the videos.

The center of the interface is dedicated to the user's workspace, where they can input their prompts and manage their creations. Below this, the library acts as a personalized repository for all videos generated by the user. It includes options to tag favorites, organize creations into folders, and upload external files for Sora to work with. These organizational tools are particularly useful for creators juggling multiple projects, as they ensure that ideas and outputs remain accessible and streamlined.

Customization is a central pillar of the Sora experience. Users can adjust parameters such as resolution, remix intensity, and the length of videos. These controls allow creators to fine-tune their outputs to meet specific needs, whether it's a quick draft at a lower resolution or a polished high-definition video for professional use. The ability to remix content and introduce minor or substantial changes provides additional flexibility, enabling creators to iterate on their ideas without starting from scratch.

At the heart of Sora's functionality is the power of prompts. Users interact with the tool by entering descriptive text into the prompt box, guiding the AI to generate video content that aligns with their vision. The level of detail in these prompts significantly impacts the results. Simple prompts can yield quick, abstract visuals, while more elaborate descriptions allow for intricate and tailored outputs. Sora's ability to interpret and creatively expand on these instructions makes it a collaborative tool, where the user's input and the AI's capabilities converge to produce compelling videos.

For example, a user might request a "sunset over a mountain range with flowing rivers and birds flying in the sky." Sora interprets this description, generating a video that reflects the user's vision while adding nuanced details such as lighting, motion, and atmospheric effects. The tool's adaptability ensures that even vague ideas can be transformed into visually engaging content, making it an ideal companion for creators at any stage of their creative process.

Through its intuitive navigation, robust features, and the dynamic interaction enabled by prompts, Sora offers a unique blend of accessibility and sophistication. It encourages exploration and experimentation, making the process of video creation not just efficient but also enjoyable and inspiring.

Sora's features, such as bookmarks, libraries, uploads, and folders, are thoughtfully integrated into its interface to enhance organization, accessibility, and creative flexibility. These tools are designed to streamline the user experience, ensuring that creators can focus on crafting compelling videos without getting lost in the technicalities of managing their projects.

Bookmarks serve as a convenient way to save and revisit prompts or creations that capture a user's interest. While exploring Sora's community-generated content or experimenting with their own prompts, users can mark specific videos that stand out or inspire them. This feature not only helps in preserving ideas for future reference but also acts as a quick-access catalog for learning from others' work. For instance, a user might bookmark a video with a particularly effective prompt to study its structure and adapt it to their own needs later.

The library is the centerpiece of personal project management within Sora. It houses all videos generated by the user, providing a centralized location to review, edit, or download content. The library's layout is designed for clarity, allowing users to quickly identify specific videos through tags or visual previews. This feature is especially useful for creators working on multiple projects, as it keeps all their outputs in one accessible space, eliminating the need to search through scattered files or folders.

The uploads feature introduces another layer of versatility. Users can import external files, such as images, to use as the foundation for their video prompts. This capability allows Sora to build upon existing visuals, adding motion, context, or enhancements based on the user's instructions. For example, a still image of a serene forest can be transformed into a dynamic video with swaying trees, cascading sunlight, and wildlife in motion. The uploads feature bridges the gap between traditional static media and the dynamic potential of AI-generated content.

Folders provide a simple yet effective way to organize projects within Sora. By categorizing videos into thematic or project-specific folders, users can maintain order and focus, even when managing extensive libraries of content. For instance, a content creator working on both marketing videos and personal art projects can separate these outputs into dedicated folders, ensuring that each remains distinct and easily accessible. This organization is particularly valuable for collaborative efforts, as it allows team members to navigate shared resources more efficiently.

Together, these features create a cohesive and user-friendly environment for video creation. Bookmarks spark inspiration and learning, libraries centralize outputs for easy management, uploads expand the scope of creative possibilities, and folders maintain order in even the busiest workflows. With these tools, Sora empowers users to navigate the complexities of video generation with simplicity and precision, transforming the creative process into an enjoyable and efficient experience.

Chapter 4: How Sora Works

The process of generating a video in Sora is both intuitive and efficient, designed to make the complex task of video creation accessible to users of all skill levels. From entering a simple text prompt to downloading a fully rendered video, Sora streamlines the workflow, allowing creators to focus on their ideas while the AI handles the technical details.

The first step in the video generation process begins with the user crafting a text prompt. This prompt serves as the guiding framework for Sora's AI, describing the desired elements, actions, or themes for the video. For instance, a user might write, "A sunset over a tropical beach with waves gently crashing on the shore." The more detailed and specific the prompt, the more refined and tailored the resulting video will be.

However, even minimal prompts can yield visually compelling results, as Sora creatively fills in gaps based on its training data.

Once the prompt is submitted, Sora processes the input and begins rendering the video. At this stage, the user can customize parameters such as resolution, video length, and remix intensity if they're revising an existing creation. These adjustments play a significant role in the final output, allowing creators to tailor the quality and scale of their videos to suit their needs.

The time it takes for Sora to generate a video depends largely on the selected resolution and the complexity of the prompt. For example:

- **Low-Resolution Videos (360p):** These are the fastest to generate, typically taking less than 20 seconds for a short clip of about five seconds. This makes them ideal for quick drafts, experimentation, or rough previews.

- **High-Resolution Videos (1080p):** These require significantly more time and computational power, especially for detailed or intricate prompts. A ten-second video at this resolution might take several minutes to render, depending on the complexity of the visual elements involved.

The rendering process occurs on OpenAI's servers, which means it is not dependent on the user's local hardware or internet speed. This cloud-based approach ensures consistent performance across devices, allowing anyone with access to Sora to create high-quality videos regardless of their technical setup.

Once the rendering is complete, the video appears in the user's library, where it can be reviewed, downloaded, or further refined. If adjustments are needed, users can either modify the original prompt or use the remix feature to make incremental changes without starting from scratch. For instance, they might enhance the resolution, alter the colors, or add new elements to an existing scene.

The efficiency of this process, combined with the creative flexibility it offers, underscores Sora's appeal as a tool for modern video creation. By balancing speed and customization, it allows users to iterate rapidly, experiment freely, and produce polished videos in a fraction of the time required by traditional methods. Whether generating a quick concept or a high-quality final product, Sora adapts seamlessly to the creator's workflow, ensuring that their vision can come to life with ease.

The storyboard feature in Sora is a powerful tool that enhances the creative process by enabling seamless transitions between scenes in a video. It addresses one of the key challenges in AI video generation—maintaining continuity and coherence across multiple prompts. By allowing users to stitch together various scenes into a unified narrative, the storyboard feature expands the possibilities of storytelling, making it particularly valuable for longer or more complex video projects.

At its core, the storyboard acts as a virtual timeline where users can arrange and connect different video segments generated from separate prompts. Each segment represents a distinct idea, action, or visual element, crafted individually within Sora's text prompt framework. For instance, a user might create one prompt for a sunrise over a forest and another for animals emerging from their habitats. The storyboard allows these scenes to flow naturally into one another, creating a cohesive progression.

Using the storyboard is straightforward. After generating the individual clips, users can drag and drop them into the timeline in their desired order. Sora's interface provides options to fine-tune the transitions between scenes, ensuring that the shift from one segment to the next feels smooth and visually consistent. This could involve blending colors, aligning motion, or adding effects that unify the overall aesthetic.

One of the storyboard's standout features is its ability to manage actions that are difficult to achieve in a single prompt. AI video generation can struggle with creating multiple actions or changes within one sequence, such as a character walking into a room, picking up an object, and exiting. The storyboard resolves this by allowing users to break the narrative into smaller, manageable pieces and then link them together in a way that maintains the illusion of continuity.

For creators aiming to produce longer videos, such as short films, presentations, or educational content, the storyboard feature is indispensable. It enables more elaborate storytelling by bridging the gaps between individual ideas and scenes. Additionally, it offers flexibility for revisions, as users can adjust the order, timing, or content of segments without needing to regenerate the entire video.

The ability to incorporate smooth scene transitions not only enhances the quality of the final output but also elevates the user's control over the creative process. By simulating the functionalities of a professional video editor, the storyboard feature transforms Sora from a simple video generation tool into a comprehensive platform for crafting dynamic and engaging visual narratives. Whether for social media clips, advertisements, or artistic projects, the storyboard empowers creators to weave their ideas together seamlessly, bringing their visions to life with precision and style.

Chapter 5: What Sora Excels At

Sora's ability to create abstract animations, along with its prowess in generating cartoon and claymation-style videos, provides users with a versatile toolkit to explore various creative avenues. These features open up possibilities for producing visually striking, non-realistic content that stands out for its artistic flair and imaginative designs.

Abstract animations represent one of the most innovative applications of Sora, allowing users to dive into a realm of creative freedom that is less tethered to realism. Through this feature, creators can generate mesmerizing visual sequences that focus on the manipulation of colors, textures, and dynamic movements, without any specific narrative or realistic representation. These animations are often experimental, often leaning into the surreal or the ethereal.

Sora's power lies in its ability to take user prompts describing abstract concepts and translate them into fluid, visually engaging animations. By requesting specific combinations of colors, shapes, or patterns, users can produce animations that resemble generative art, fluid dynamics, or even psychedelic visuals. Imagine a video of shifting gradients or morphing geometric shapes—these abstract sequences can serve as background visuals for music videos, digital art exhibitions, or even as hypnotic screensavers.

The texturing capabilities of Sora allow users to create intricate surfaces that feel tactile despite their lack of representation in the real world. For example, users can generate animations featuring liquid-like textures that ripple and swirl, mimicking the behaviors of water, ink, or molten metal. These abstract animations can vary in complexity, with some focusing on smooth transitions of hues and others pushing the boundaries into more chaotic and unpredictable designs.

For creators interested in minimalist art or those seeking a modern aesthetic, abstract animations become a canvas for pure imagination. The ability to control the flow of colors and textures opens up endless creative potential for projects that require stunning visual elements that don't need to follow the rules of the natural world. Whether used as atmospheric footage or as an attention-grabbing visual, abstract animations generated by Sora can serve as an essential tool for anyone working in the realms of digital media and creative visual storytelling.

The cartoon and claymation-style video generation is another area where Sora shines, offering a unique alternative to photorealistic content. These styles are particularly valuable for creators aiming to produce videos that convey personality, creativity, and humor, without the limitations of natural physics or realistic movement. They provide a platform for more playful, experimental, and highly stylized content that appeals to a broad audience.

Cartoon-style videos generated by Sora can range from simple 2D animations to more complex 3D renderings. The charm of cartoon-style visuals lies in their exaggerated and abstract representations of characters, actions, and environments. Unlike traditional AI-generated photorealistic images or videos that struggle with object permanence and movement, cartoon videos often sidestep these issues entirely because the aesthetic does not demand realism. The characters, objects, and actions in these videos adhere to a stylized logic rather than a natural one. This flexibility allows Sora to produce highly engaging and often whimsical content that resonates with viewers on an emotional and imaginative level.

Whether the goal is to create a playful animation for children, a quirky ad, or even a satirical take on real-world events, the cartoon style provides the freedom to bend the rules of visual storytelling. The charm of these animations lies in their intentional departure from reality, creating characters that might have exaggerated features, like oversized heads or impossibly large eyes, and environments that bend and twist in ways the real world cannot.

Similarly, claymation-style videos offer a nostalgic throwback to traditional stop-motion animation, but with the speed and ease of AI generation. This style, reminiscent of beloved clay-animated films, brings characters and objects to life in a way that feels tactile and handcrafted, even though the process is entirely digital. Sora can generate these types of animations by simulating the stop-motion process, where figures appear to move frame by frame, just like in traditional claymation. However, unlike traditional stop-motion, Sora's technology enables faster production, making it accessible to anyone looking to create these unique animations without the labor-intensive process.

The appeal of claymation lies in its warmth and the handmade, often quirky nature of its characters. It gives creators the opportunity to produce short films, advertisements, or social media content that carry the distinctive charm of handcrafted animation. This style also lends itself well to projects that aim to tell stories with humor or whimsy, making it ideal for brands and creators targeting a younger audience or those looking to bring a playful touch to their messaging.

In both cartoon and claymation styles, Sora offers a canvas that is less constrained by the technical limitations of more photorealistic video generation. Errors in physics, object movement, or character interaction become less noticeable because the visual language of these styles does not require strict adherence to the rules of the real world. This makes Sora particularly well-suited for creators who are more focused on the aesthetic and artistic expression rather than photorealism or perfect continuity.

These styles are also highly adaptable, allowing for experimentation with different visual elements. A user might start with a basic cartoon character and then change its environment, actions, or color palette to suit the mood or tone of the video. Similarly, a claymation scene can be adjusted to feature different characters or settings, giving creators endless options for storytelling within a more abstract and fun-filled framework.

In summary, Sora's capabilities in abstract animation and cartoon/claymation-style video generation offer creators a playground of possibilities. Whether you're seeking to create visually stunning abstract backgrounds, engaging animated characters, or nostalgic claymation-inspired videos, Sora provides the tools to bring these creative visions to life with ease. These features allow for both experimentation and creativity, making them invaluable for anyone looking to push the boundaries of AI-generated video content.

Sora's ability to integrate text into videos adds a layer of functionality that is both practical and visually impactful. Whether used for titles, slides, or captions, text integration is a crucial element for creators looking to convey information, establish context, or enhance the storytelling aspect of their videos. Alongside this, Sora's penchant for taking creative liberties—such as adding unexpected objects or styles—introduces an element of spontaneity and surprise, making the tool a dynamic partner in the creative process.

Text integration within Sora is more than a simple overlay of words onto a visual background. The tool is capable of embedding text in a way that feels organic to the video's style, mood, and overall aesthetic. Users can request specific fonts, colors, and placements, resulting in text that harmonizes seamlessly with the visual elements of the scene. For instance, a creator might ask for a hand-drawn font style to complement a sketch-like animation or bold, modern typography to align with a futuristic theme.

One of Sora's strengths in this area is its ability to animate text, creating dynamic effects such as letters appearing one by one, fading in and out, or moving along a specific path. These animations can turn otherwise static title slides into engaging introductory sequences, ideal for presentations, documentaries, or branded content. For example, a user might prompt Sora to sketch the Empire State Building while incorporating the title of a video about New York

City. The result would be a cohesive blend of animated visuals and text, setting the tone for the content that follows.

Sora also demonstrates increasing accuracy when generating text directly requested by the user. While earlier iterations sometimes produced garbled or nonsensical words, the tool now performs well when asked to create specific titles or labels. This improvement makes Sora particularly useful for creating polished, professional-looking slides for educational or marketing purposes. The ability to visually customize text ensures that creators can match the tone of their content, whether it's playful, formal, or experimental.

In addition, text integration within videos isn't limited to straightforward use cases like titles. Sora can incorporate text into the environment itself, blending it with the scene as if it were a natural part of the surroundings. For instance, a video of a street might include graffiti on a wall with a user-specified message or advertisement. This capability offers creators a unique way to integrate messaging into their visuals, making the text feel immersive and part of the story.

One of the most intriguing aspects of working with Sora is its tendency to take creative liberties, introducing unexpected elements or styles that weren't explicitly requested in the user's prompt. While these additions can sometimes be surprising, they often enhance the video in ways that spark further creativity or offer inspiration for new ideas.

For instance, users have noted that Sora might add a decorative object, such as a plant or lamp, to a scene without being asked. These additions, while not central to the requested content, often add depth and realism to the video. In one example, a user requesting a video of a tech reviewer at a desk found that Sora had included a detailed fake plant in the background. While this wasn't part of the original prompt, it enriched the scene, adding an extra layer of visual interest.

Sora's creative liberties extend to stylistic choices as well. It might interpret a user's prompt in ways that push beyond the literal, introducing visual effects or design elements that enhance the overall aesthetic. For example, when asked to create a video of Santa fighting Frosty the Snowman in the style of a video game, Sora not only delivered the requested action but also included a functional-looking scoreboard. This unprompted detail contributed to the authenticity of the scene, making it feel like an actual gaming experience.

These moments of spontaneity highlight Sora's strength as a collaborative tool rather than a mere executor of instructions. While users retain control over the overall direction of their videos, Sora's ability to fill in gaps with its own creative decisions can lead to results that are richer and more engaging than anticipated. For creators, this adds an element of discovery to the process, as they explore how the tool interprets their vision.

However, these liberties also underscore the importance of iteration and refinement. While some unexpected elements may enhance the video, others might require adjustment or removal to align with the creator's intent. Fortunately, Sora's remix feature makes it easy to revise these outputs, allowing users to refine the level of creativity or randomness included in their videos.

Together, Sora's text integration capabilities and its creative unpredictability make it a versatile and inspiring tool for video creation. Whether crafting precise, professional slides or experimenting with imaginative visuals, creators can rely on Sora to deliver results that are both functional and visually compelling. Its combination of structured text handling and artistic spontaneity ensures that every project has the potential to surprise, delight, and captivate its audience.

Chapter 6: The Strength of Imagination

Sora's remixing features and its ability to handle surreal or conceptual prompts are two standout capabilities that amplify its creative potential. These features allow users to refine their ideas, iterate on existing content, and explore the boundaries of imagination, making Sora a dynamic tool for both precision and experimentation.

The remixing feature in Sora is a powerful tool that enables users to modify and enhance previously generated videos without starting from scratch. This functionality is especially useful for creators who want to build on a base concept or refine details in their videos. By adjusting specific aspects of an existing creation, users can experiment with new ideas, correct errors, or adapt content for different purposes.

Remixing begins by selecting a video from the library and specifying the desired changes. These can range from subtle tweaks, such as altering the color scheme or resolution, to more significant transformations, like changing the setting or adding new elements. For instance, a user might start with a video of a serene mountain landscape and then remix it to include a golf course in the background. Sora processes these instructions and generates an updated version of the video, retaining the core elements while incorporating the requested modifications.

A key feature of the remixing tool is its customizable intensity slider, which allows users to control the degree of change. Whether the adjustment is mild, moderate, or dramatic, the slider provides a nuanced way to guide Sora's reinterpretation of the original video. This flexibility ensures that creators can achieve their desired results, whether they're fine-tuning details or pursuing a bold new direction.

The remixing feature is also time-efficient. Instead of generating an entirely new video from a fresh prompt, remixing focuses on targeted changes, reducing rendering times and allowing for quicker iterations. This makes it ideal for creators who want to test multiple variations of a concept or respond to feedback in real time.

Sora's ability to interpret and execute surreal or conceptual prompts highlights its role as a tool for pushing creative boundaries. Unlike traditional video creation methods that rely on realism or linear storytelling, Sora excels at bringing abstract, imaginative ideas to life. This makes it particularly appealing to artists, content creators, and visionaries looking to explore uncharted visual territories.

Surreal prompts challenge Sora to blend the unexpected, creating visuals that defy logic or conventional representation. For example, a user might request a video of "a clock made of melting ice floating in a desert under a pink sky." Sora interprets such inputs to generate videos that merge disparate elements into a cohesive, dreamlike scene. These outputs often evoke a sense of wonder and intrigue, offering unique possibilities for projects that aim to captivate or provoke thought.

Conceptual prompts, on the other hand, focus on abstract themes or ideas rather than concrete visuals. A prompt like "the feeling of nostalgia visualized as moving waves of light" challenges Sora to represent emotions or concepts through creative use of color, motion, and texture. These videos can be deeply evocative, serving as artistic expressions or even meditative experiences.

Experimentation with surreal and conceptual prompts is also a way to discover Sora's creative potential. Users often find that the tool introduces unexpected details or interpretations that enrich the final result. For instance, in response to a surreal prompt, Sora might add stylistic flourishes, such as swirling patterns or glowing elements, that enhance the video's impact.

The ability to handle these unconventional ideas makes Sora a valuable resource for exploring the boundaries of imagination. It offers a platform for creators to visualize concepts that might be difficult or impossible to produce using traditional methods. Whether for art installations, digital exhibitions, or personal projects, Sora's interpretations of surreal and conceptual prompts provide endless opportunities for creativity.

In essence, Sora's remixing features and its capacity to handle surreal and conceptual prompts empower users to refine their work and push creative limits. By enabling both precision and experimentation, these capabilities make Sora an indispensable tool for anyone seeking to create content that is as unique as it is innovative. Whether building on existing ideas or venturing into the unknown, Sora provides the tools to turn visions into captivating reality.

Sora's capacity to generate artistic and non-realistic outputs positions it as a versatile tool for creators who seek to explore unconventional visual storytelling. This feature provides a playground for imaginative experimentation, allowing users to transcend the boundaries of realism and produce content that is striking, innovative, and deeply expressive. By embracing the abstract, surreal, or stylized, Sora empowers creators to craft visuals that evoke emotion, provoke thought, and stand out in an increasingly saturated digital landscape.

Artistic outputs in Sora are not constrained by the need to mimic reality. Instead, they focus on capturing mood, tone, and aesthetic through creative use of colors, shapes, and movement. For example, a user might request a video of "a city skyline that transforms into cascading ribbons of light." Sora interprets such prompts by blending familiar elements with fantastical ones, creating a visual narrative that feels fluid and dreamlike. These outputs can range from visually soothing to dramatically intense, depending on the user's instructions.

The tool's ability to generate non-realistic visuals also makes it a powerful resource for conceptual and experimental art. Whether it's crafting animated abstract forms, morphing geometric patterns, or surreal landscapes, Sora's flexibility allows creators to push beyond traditional artistic conventions. This can result in unique visuals that feel more like living pieces of art than conventional video clips.

Sora's strength in this area lies in its capacity to adapt to a wide variety of styles and themes. A single prompt can yield outputs reminiscent of watercolor paintings, digital glitch art, or even claymation-like textures. This adaptability allows users to tailor the tool's artistic direction to suit their projects. For instance, an animator might use Sora to generate quirky, cartoonish visuals for a children's story, while a digital artist might explore abstract animations for a music video or art installation.

The non-realistic capabilities of Sora also open up opportunities for projects that require a high degree of creative flexibility. Advertisements, for example, can benefit from eye-catching, surreal visuals that grab attention and convey brand messaging in unconventional ways. Similarly, social media content creators can use Sora to craft short, visually engaging clips that stand out in a sea of conventional videos.

One of the most exciting aspects of Sora's artistic and non-realistic outputs is the freedom it offers users to experiment without fear of constraints. Unlike traditional video production, which often requires precision and adherence to physical rules, Sora thrives in an environment where imagination is the only limit. This makes it an ideal tool for creators who wish to explore new ideas, test unconventional concepts, or simply play with visual aesthetics for inspiration.

For creators seeking maximum creative flexibility, Sora becomes a collaborative partner in artistic exploration. By generating content that defies traditional boundaries, it encourages users to think outside the box and embrace the unexpected. The resulting visuals are not only visually stunning but also deeply reflective of the creator's unique vision, making them ideal for projects that demand originality and impact.

Chapter 7: Where Sora Falls Short

One of the most prominent challenges in AI-generated video, particularly with tools like Sora, is the issue of **object permanence**. In traditional video production, whether through animation, live-action, or CGI, objects within a scene must maintain their presence and consistency across frames. For AI tools, this is a much more difficult task, as they need to simulate continuity over time, ensuring that objects don't randomly appear or disappear, and that they interact with their environment in a believable way.

Object permanence refers to the AI's ability to remember and maintain objects across multiple frames of a video. In real-world video creation, once an object enters a scene, it must remain in view until it logically exits or is obscured by another object. However, AI-generated videos often struggle with this concept. A common problem in Sora is that objects within the scene can mysteriously disappear or reappear, seemingly without reason. For instance, a character in a video might be holding an object one moment, only for it to vanish in the next frame. Similarly, an object in the background could suddenly fade out of view or pop back into existence with no logical explanation.

These kinds of inconsistencies break the immersion of the video, making it clear to viewers that what they are watching is not a fully realized, human-created production. The disappearance of objects or sudden, unprompted reappearance of elements can undermine the believability of the video, especially in more complex or realistic scenes. The challenge here is rooted in the AI's inability to truly "remember" and track objects in the same way that humans do, leading to moments of disorientation or surprise that are unintended.

Another major hurdle in AI-generated video is **realistic physics and movement**. While creating static images allows AI to focus solely on visual fidelity, generating realistic motion introduces a host of additional challenges. In realistic video production, movement must adhere to the principles of physics: gravity, inertia, friction, and so on. For AI systems like Sora, replicating these physical dynamics is still an imperfect process.

One of the most common errors is related to the movement of characters, particularly when it comes to walking. In AI-generated videos, especially those attempting to mimic photorealism, human figures or animals often exhibit erratic or unnatural walking cycles. For example, a person might appear to walk normally in one frame, but upon closer inspection, the legs might switch positions randomly or become disjointed, with the front leg turning into the back leg. These inconsistencies in walking mechanics are jarring, as our brains are incredibly sensitive to natural movement, and even slight irregularities are noticeable.

In addition to walking errors, another issue arises in the **inconsistent speed** of movements. In traditional video, characters or objects move at a constant or logically accelerating rate, based on the action being portrayed. However, AI-generated video often shows characters moving at inconsistent speeds, with actions that begin too fast or slow down inexplicably. For example, a person walking may suddenly move at a much faster pace in one frame and then slow down dramatically in the next. These abrupt changes in speed disrupt the flow of the scene and remind viewers that the video is a result of AI processing, not natural human motion.

Sora's AI attempts to generate the continuity of movement by stringing together individual frames, but the transition between them can lack the fluidity and precision of true animation or live-action filming. This results in unnatural motion, especially when dealing with complex actions that involve multiple objects or characters interacting with each other in real-time.

The issues of object permanence and realistic physics in AI-generated video are not unique to Sora—most AI video generation tools face similar challenges. These problems arise because the AI does not have an inherent understanding of the world's physical rules or a true sense of continuity. Instead, it relies on training data and learned patterns to generate each frame independently, often with errors in the transitions between them.

However, as AI continues to improve, solutions to these challenges are on the horizon. Future iterations of Sora and other video generation tools will likely enhance their ability to track objects more effectively and generate smoother, more realistic movement. In the meantime, users can work around these issues by focusing on abstract or non-realistic content, where inconsistencies in movement and object permanence are less noticeable and don't detract from the overall experience.

In summary, while Sora is an incredible tool for generating video content quickly and creatively, its challenges with object permanence and realistic physics highlight the current limitations of AI-driven video production. These imperfections may be evident to viewers but can also be a source of inspiration for creators exploring more stylized, abstract, or whimsical visuals that don't rely on perfect realism. As AI video generation technology evolves, we can expect these issues to diminish, but for now, they serve as a reminder of the evolving nature of this innovative field.

The struggle with **photorealism** and **human-like video generation** remains one of the most significant challenges for AI-driven video tools, including Sora. While advancements in AI have allowed for impressive results in image generation, extending this level of realism to video—especially when it involves human figures and complex interactions—introduces a host of technical and conceptual hurdles that the current technology has yet to fully overcome.

Photorealism is the art of creating images or videos that are indistinguishable from real life, where every detail—from lighting and textures to shadows and reflections—mimics the natural world with incredible accuracy. In the case of AI-generated video, achieving photorealism requires the system to understand not just the objects and their relationships within a scene, but also how these elements behave over time. This is particularly challenging because video involves dynamic movement, lighting changes, and interactions between multiple objects or characters—all of which must be rendered with perfect consistency across frames.

For Sora, achieving photorealism involves generating individual frames that each appear lifelike. However, the AI struggles with maintaining this level of detail consistently throughout a video. For instance, while Sora may be able to generate a single, highly detailed frame of a human character in a lifelike environment, the subsequent frames can often break this illusion. The transition from one frame to the next may not account for subtle changes in lighting, texture, or the fine details that make the scene look real. This can result in jarring inconsistencies, such as sudden shifts in color, lighting, or the appearance of objects that disrupt the overall realism of the video.

In addition, the AI's understanding of textures, such as skin, hair, or fabric, is still imperfect. Small imperfections—such as unnatural reflections on skin or hair that doesn't behave as it should in motion—are common. These details, while subtle, contribute significantly to the believability of a photorealistic video. The current limitations of AI-driven video generation tools like Sora mean that these imperfections often break the illusion, reminding the viewer that they are watching a computer-generated video rather than real footage.

Generating **human-like movement** is another area where Sora, and similar AI video generation tools, face significant challenges. Humans are highly complex in their physical movements—our bodies are capable of nuanced, coordinated actions that are difficult for AI to replicate convincingly. From walking and talking to more intricate gestures, human movements are governed by subtle shifts in muscle tension, balance, and natural rhythm. Replicating this level of detail within an AI-generated video is a complex task, and as of now, Sora struggles with several aspects of human-like video generation.

One of the most common issues with human-like movement is **inconsistent or unrealistic walking cycles**. In many AI-generated videos, human figures may appear to walk, but upon close inspection, their leg movements seem unnatural. For instance, the movement of the legs may not follow a natural gait—front and back legs might appear to switch roles, or the rhythm of the steps may suddenly speed up or slow down for no reason. These inconsistencies in walking and body mechanics are noticeable to viewers, disrupting the flow of the scene and undermining the realism of the video.

Moreover, **facial expressions** and **lip syncing** remain areas of struggle for AI video generation. While AI can produce faces with impressive detail, the subtleties of human expression—such as slight shifts in emotion or the coordination of facial muscles—are often missing or exaggerated.

In videos where characters are speaking, the synchronization of lip movement with the audio can also be off, creating a disconnect between the character's appearance and the sound. These issues arise because Sora doesn't possess a true understanding of the human body and how it moves; instead, it relies on learned patterns and datasets to approximate human movement, which often leads to errors in fluidity and realism.

Another challenge is **emotion and body language**. Human communication relies heavily on non-verbal cues—slight gestures, postures, and micro-expressions—that convey meaning. AI has difficulty understanding and reproducing these subtle cues in a natural way. While Sora may generate a human figure that looks realistic in isolation, the character's actions and expressions can feel stiff or exaggerated, failing to capture the nuances that make human communication so dynamic.

Despite these challenges, Sora and other AI tools are continuously improving. Advances in deep learning and machine vision are slowly bridging the gap between artificial and natural realism. AI models are increasingly capable of generating higher-quality textures, smoother movements, and more consistent visual continuity. As these models train on larger, more diverse datasets and improve their understanding of human behavior, it is likely that the photorealism and human-like video generation will continue to improve.

However, it's important to recognize that achieving perfect photorealism in AI video is not an immediate goal. As of now, the focus is often on creative flexibility, allowing users to explore more stylized or abstract video outputs, where the imperfections in realism become less noticeable or even desirable. For creators who are not focused on replicating real-life scenarios, but instead wish to explore imaginative, conceptual, or non-realistic content, Sora's imperfections can become part of the creative process. The tool's strength lies in its ability to offer freedom and flexibility for artistic exploration, even if it isn't yet capable of perfect human-like video generation.

In conclusion, while Sora's struggles with photorealism and human-like video generation are significant limitations, they also highlight the evolving nature of AI-driven video technology. As the field progresses, these challenges will likely be addressed, bringing us closer to fully immersive, lifelike AI-generated content. Until then, Sora remains a powerful tool for creators looking to explore new artistic frontiers, even if it's still working to perfect the complexities of realism and human-like movement.

Chapter 8: Ethical and Technical Concerns

As AI-generated content becomes more prevalent, **copyright and intellectual property (IP) challenges** have emerged as significant concerns for both creators and developers of these technologies. When it comes to tools like Sora by OpenAI, the issues surrounding IP ownership, ethical usage, and the protection of rights are not only legal in nature but also integral to how the platform is structured and used by individuals worldwide.

One of the most pressing concerns with AI-generated content is determining who holds the rights to the videos or images produced. Traditionally, intellectual property laws are built around the concept of human authorship—where the creator of a work holds the rights to that work. However, when an AI tool is used to generate content, the situation becomes more complicated. Since Sora, and similar AI systems, generate content without direct human authorship in the traditional sense, questions arise about who owns the rights to the videos generated.

While users of Sora are typically allowed to use and publish the content they create, the ownership of these creations can be murky. In general, OpenAI's terms of service likely outline the specific rights granted to users, stating that users retain the rights to their generated videos, but OpenAI may still have certain rights to the underlying data and algorithms used to create the content. This means that while you may own the rights to a video you create using Sora, there could still be restrictions related to how the AI was trained or the data used to develop it.

A significant **limitation imposed by AI platforms like Sora** is the inability to generate content that includes **recognizable public figures**, such as celebrities, politicians, or other well-known personalities, without proper authorization. This is due to the potential **violation of personality rights**, which protect individuals from unauthorized commercial use of their likenesses or identity.

For example, Sora users cannot legally create a video featuring a recognizable image or likeness of someone like Beyoncé or Elon Musk unless they have the rights or consent to do so. Even if the AI tool generates a convincing imitation of a public figure, this could still result in legal challenges, as the individual's right to their likeness is protected by law in many jurisdictions.

Similarly, **copyrighted material**, including images, videos, music, and text from protected works, cannot be generated or incorporated into new AI-created content unless the creator has explicit permission or the material is in the public domain. This means that even if Sora can generate a video that closely resembles scenes from a popular movie or TV show, doing so without obtaining the proper rights would violate copyright law. This restriction is important not only to prevent legal issues but also to ensure that AI-generated content does not inadvertently infringe on the intellectual property of creators who hold rights to specific works.

To mitigate these risks and ensure that its tools are used ethically and legally, OpenAI has implemented a number of **guardrails and restrictions** around the usage of Sora. These safeguards are designed to prevent misuse of the platform while promoting ethical and responsible content creation.

1. **Content Moderation and Filtering:** OpenAI has likely integrated content moderation systems within Sora to automatically flag or prevent the generation of content that violates its terms of service. This includes content that may be offensive, harmful, or in violation of IP laws. For example, users cannot generate violent, discriminatory, or harmful imagery, and AI-generated content that closely resembles copyrighted works or likenesses of public figures may be blocked or flagged for review.

2. **Ethical Use Guidelines:** OpenAI has also set ethical use guidelines for Sora,

ensuring that the platform is used to create content that aligns with legal standards and does not cause harm. These guidelines likely cover areas such as the creation of deepfakes, misleading videos, or other types of disinformation. The goal is to prevent AI tools like Sora from being used to create content that could be harmful to individuals or society, such as fake news or manipulative media.

3. **Preventing Plagiarism:** Sora's algorithms are designed to generate new content based on user input rather than directly replicating existing works. While this feature allows for creative flexibility, it also means that users cannot simply reproduce or steal someone else's intellectual property. OpenAI has likely built safeguards into Sora that limit the tool's

ability to directly replicate copyrighted images or videos. This helps ensure that users are not inadvertently infringing on others' IP rights.

4. **Educational Content and Transparency:** OpenAI places a strong emphasis on educating users about ethical content creation. In addition to implementing restrictions, OpenAI often provides clear documentation, tutorials, and resources to help creators understand how to use Sora responsibly. This includes guidance on respecting intellectual property rights, avoiding plagiarism, and understanding the ethical implications of AI-generated content.

5. **Licensing and Commercial Use:** For users who intend to use AI-generated content for commercial purposes, such as

marketing, advertisements, or product creation, OpenAI may have additional licensing agreements or restrictions. These may require users to explicitly confirm that they have the right to use the generated content for commercial purposes and that the content complies with all copyright laws and ethical guidelines.

As AI technology continues to advance, the relationship between AI-generated content and intellectual property law will evolve. Currently, many aspects of copyright law struggle to keep pace with the rapid development of AI tools. For instance, who owns a work created by an AI system that is trained on vast datasets containing copyrighted materials? Should the AI itself have any rights, or should the human users be granted full ownership of the content they create using these tools? These are open questions that will require ongoing legal and ethical debate.

There may also be calls for new **legislation** or **regulations** that specifically address AI and IP concerns, providing clearer guidelines on how AI-generated content is treated under copyright law. Until then, both AI developers like OpenAI and users must remain vigilant about respecting intellectual property rights and ensuring that the content created with AI tools does not infringe on the rights of others.

The **copyright and intellectual property challenges** surrounding Sora and similar AI tools reflect the growing complexity of using artificial intelligence to create media. While OpenAI has taken steps to impose ethical usage restrictions and ensure that its AI tools are used legally and responsibly, there is still much to navigate in terms of ownership, licensing, and the protection of rights. By understanding these limitations and adhering to the ethical guidelines set by OpenAI, creators can explore the powerful capabilities of AI video generation while minimizing the risk of legal and ethical violations. As AI technology continues to evolve, these challenges will undoubtedly shape the future of creative media and content generation.

Chapter 9: Practical Applications

Creators today have a wealth of opportunities to leverage Sora's capabilities in various contexts, from personal projects to commercial use. The power of AI-driven video generation enables creators to produce content that is visually engaging and innovative, pushing the boundaries of traditional video creation. Here's how Sora can be used in real-world applications:

Social Media is one of the primary platforms where creators can maximize the potential of Sora. With the increasing demand for engaging and dynamic video content, Sora's AI tools can generate videos that captivate audiences in ways that static images or basic animations cannot. Creators can generate short videos for Instagram stories, TikTok clips, YouTube Shorts, or other social media platforms, allowing them to keep up with the fast-paced content cycle while maintaining high creativity and production quality.

For **advertisements**, Sora provides an efficient and cost-effective way to produce promotional videos. Whether for a small business or a large brand, marketers can use Sora to create eye-catching, customized ads. The ability to experiment with different video styles, from photorealistic to abstract, allows for tailored advertisements that align with brand identity, making campaigns stand out in a crowded market.

Additionally, **experimental projects** are another area where Sora excels. Since it allows for significant creative freedom, artists and creators can explore unconventional video styles that are not bound by traditional production methods.

Whether it's creating surreal landscapes, fantastical creatures, or entirely new video formats, Sora's AI can be used to push the boundaries of what's possible, making it an ideal tool for experimental video creation.

One of the exciting things about Sora is its ability to generate **abstract art** and **creative visuals**. For digital artists or content creators working in industries like design or entertainment, Sora offers a unique way to create abstract animations, textures, and color patterns. These can be used as standalone pieces of art or as part of a larger video project, adding depth and creativity that may not be easily achievable through traditional methods.

For **title slides** and **opening sequences**, Sora can create dynamic and attention-grabbing video intros. This is especially useful for YouTube creators, podcasters, or anyone producing long-form video content. Instead of relying on basic, pre-made templates, creators can generate highly customized, AI-powered title slides that match the tone and style of their content, making their videos more professional and engaging.

Background animations are another practical use of Sora's capabilities. Whether for websites, presentations, or video productions, creators can use Sora to generate looping background animations that complement the content without overwhelming it. These could range from abstract patterns to simple animated landscapes, providing the perfect visual setting for other elements like text or images in a video.

In all of these use cases, Sora allows creators to **streamline the video production process** while still offering ample creative control. By tapping into the vast potential of AI video generation, creators can produce professional-quality content quickly and with a level of creativity that might not be possible using traditional video editing tools. The flexibility in style, design, and animation possibilities makes Sora a versatile tool for both personal and professional projects.

Chapter 10: The Implications of AI Video Generation

The advent of AI video generation, particularly through tools like Sora, has brought about a shift in how content is created and perceived. While the technology opens up incredible opportunities for innovation, it also raises important questions regarding **content authenticity** and **trust**.

As AI-generated content becomes more sophisticated, distinguishing between real and artificial videos becomes increasingly difficult. This blurring of lines between authentic and generated content can erode **trust** in visual media. With the ability to create highly realistic videos or manipulate existing footage, there's a growing concern over misinformation, deepfakes, and other forms of deceptive media.

For instance, AI could be used to create videos of public figures or fake events, which, without proper verification, could mislead viewers.

On the flip side, **authenticity** is key for creators who use AI responsibly. By openly acknowledging the use of AI in their work and being transparent about the creation process, creators can build trust with their audience. Still, the sheer volume of content generated by AI makes it harder for audiences to critically assess the authenticity of what they see online, potentially diminishing the perceived value of content over time.

The ability to produce unique and imaginative content through AI like Sora presents enormous opportunities for **innovation**. Artists, educators, marketers, and even scientists can harness AI to experiment with new creative forms, revolutionizing industries like advertising, entertainment, and education. Video production becomes faster, cheaper, and more customizable, empowering creators from diverse fields to engage audiences in novel ways.

However, this innovation also comes with significant **risks of misuse**. As AI-generated content becomes more accessible, malicious actors could exploit these tools to produce harmful content, such as fake news, propaganda, or unethical deepfakes. The line between what's real and what's generated could become dangerously blurred, leading to challenges in combating disinformation. Without appropriate regulations and safeguards, the misuse of AI in media could have far-reaching consequences for society, especially when it comes to issues like privacy and intellectual property.

To combat the growing challenge of distinguishing AI-generated content from human-created content, many platforms and tools, including Sora, are incorporating **watermarking** features. Watermarks are embedded in AI-generated videos to indicate their artificial origins, providing a layer of **transparency** for viewers. This helps creators and platforms ensure that the content's AI-driven nature is clear, making it easier for audiences to understand that what they're watching is computer-generated rather than authentic.

While watermarking is a useful tool, it is not a foolproof solution. Watermarks can sometimes be **removed** or altered, either by tech-savvy users or by other AI systems designed to do so. In addition, not all platforms require watermarks, and some videos may circulate without them, further complicating efforts to maintain content authenticity. Moreover, watermarking doesn't address the underlying issue of trust in the content itself—it only identifies the medium used to create it. Therefore, while watermarking is an important step, it needs to be part of a broader effort to establish ethical guidelines and technology-driven solutions to protect against misuse.

In summary, while AI video generation tools like Sora offer vast potential for creativity and innovation, they also introduce significant challenges around content authenticity, trust, and misuse. By implementing safeguards like watermarking and fostering transparent communication, creators and platforms can help ensure that AI-generated content is used responsibly, while mitigating the risks associated with its abuse. The ultimate goal is to find a balance where AI enhances creativity and efficiency, without compromising the integrity of content in a world where trust is paramount.

Chapter 11: The Future of Sora and AI-Generated Media

As we look to the future of AI video tools like **Sora**, several key developments are expected to shape not just the technology itself, but also the industries and society at large. The evolution of these tools will continue to accelerate, and with it, the creative landscape will undergo profound changes, creating both opportunities and challenges.

In the near future, it's likely that **Sora** will continue to evolve, refining its capabilities and expanding its range of features. As AI technology advances, we can expect the following developments:

1. **Increased Realism and Precision**: As AI models are trained on increasingly diverse and high-quality datasets, the realism of

AI-generated videos will improve. This means fewer glitches, smoother transitions, and more lifelike animations. Sora may soon be able to generate videos that are indistinguishable from human-created content in terms of both quality and style, especially in areas like human movement and facial expressions, which remain a challenge for current AI systems.

2. **Expanded Creative Flexibility**: Sora's ability to produce abstract, surreal, and stylized videos will continue to evolve, giving creators even more flexibility in their visual expression. Advanced AI models could allow users to experiment with entirely new visual styles, genres, and formats, taking creativity to uncharted territories. New features may also allow

for better integration of sound, movement, and narrative, leading to more immersive and dynamic video creation tools.

3. **Improved Customization and Interactivity**: As Sora becomes more accessible to a wider range of users, we may see features that allow for deeper customization. This could include the ability to fine-tune video elements such as character emotions, voiceovers, and scene pacing with even more precision. The interface may also become more intuitive, allowing even novice users to create high-quality content without steep learning curves.

4. **AI-Assisted Editing and Post-Production**: AI could soon play a bigger role in the post-production process as well, offering automatic edits, color grading, and even

sound design based on the user's preferences or creative direction. This would streamline the entire video creation process, reducing the need for manual labor and allowing creators to focus more on their ideas.

5. **Integration with Other AI Tools**: The future of Sora and similar AI platforms will likely see greater integration with other AI tools for seamless workflows. For instance, users might be able to easily incorporate AI-generated music, scripts, or sound effects into their videos, resulting in a fully AI-assisted production pipeline. This would enable even greater creative expression and speed up the video creation process across industries.

As tools like Sora become more widely available, their **accessibility** will have a profound impact on creative industries. Currently, video production requires significant expertise, resources, and time—especially for high-quality content. With the rise of AI tools, the barriers to entry are rapidly lowering, allowing creators of all skill levels to produce professional-grade videos from the comfort of their own homes.

This democratization of video creation will lead to a **shift in power dynamics** within creative fields. Traditionally, large studios and production companies had control over media content, but as AI video tools become more accessible, independent creators, small businesses, and even hobbyists will have the ability to produce high-quality content at a fraction of the cost. This is likely to disrupt industries such as advertising, film, and content creation, leading to more diverse voices and perspectives in media.

However, this shift also presents challenges. As more people create content using AI, there could be an **over saturation** of media, making it more difficult for individual creators to stand out. In addition, there may be increasing pressure on professionals in fields like video editing, animation, and graphic design, as AI tools like Sora continue to automate tasks that once required specialized skills.

In the short term, we might see industries like **social media** and **advertising** become even more reliant on AI-generated content, particularly as companies seek to engage with audiences in new and innovative ways. **Marketing campaigns** that use customized, AI-generated videos to target specific audiences will likely become a standard practice, allowing brands to produce content at scale while still maintaining personalization.

The rise of AI tools in video creation will have broader societal implications, particularly in how we **perceive reality** and interact with media. AI-generated videos are poised to challenge the very nature of truth in visual media, particularly as the technology continues to improve.

1. **The Impact on Trust**: As AI-generated content becomes indistinguishable from real-world footage, the public's trust in visual media could erode. Just as digital manipulation of photos and videos has become a common practice, the ability to create entirely artificial videos will make it even harder to distinguish fact from fiction. Deepfakes, for example, already pose a significant challenge to the integrity of media, and the advent of highly realistic AI-generated videos could further fuel concerns about the

manipulation of public opinion and political discourse.

2. **Redefining Media Consumption**: With AI-generated content flooding the media landscape, viewers will need to develop new skills to critically assess what they are consuming. The traditional roles of journalists, content creators, and media producers may be altered, as AI-generated content takes up a larger share of the media landscape. This will necessitate the development of new tools for media literacy and the implementation of regulations to help distinguish between authentic and AI-generated content.

3. **Cultural Shifts in Creativity**: AI video tools are also likely to shift the way we think about **creativity**. In the past, creativity has been associated with human

intuition, emotion, and originality. However, as AI becomes better at replicating these aspects of creativity, it raises philosophical questions about whether something created by a machine can truly be considered "art." This could lead to a **redefinition of creativity**, where human input and machine output are seen as complementary rather than in opposition.

4. **The Future of Employment in Creative Fields**: The proliferation of AI tools in creative industries could lead to significant changes in the job market. While AI will certainly create new roles—such as AI trainers, curators, or ethics specialists—it may also render some traditional creative jobs obsolete. Video editors, animators, and content producers

may find themselves facing competition from AI tools that can perform their tasks more efficiently, sparking debates about the future of work in creative industries.

5. **Ethical Dilemmas and Responsibility**: The widespread use of AI in video generation will undoubtedly raise **ethical questions**. Who is responsible for AI-generated content? If an AI creates a controversial video, who should be held accountable—the creator, the platform, or the developers behind the AI? How can we ensure that AI is not used to create harmful content, such as propaganda or hate speech? These questions will need to be addressed as AI tools continue to evolve.

The future of AI video tools like Sora is incredibly exciting, with potential for groundbreaking innovation and creativity. However, these developments will also come with significant societal implications, from shifting power dynamics in the creative industries to challenging the very nature of truth and authenticity in media. As we navigate this new era, it will be crucial to balance the incredible potential of AI with the need for ethical guidelines, transparency, and a commitment to maintaining trust in the media we consume. The role of AI in shaping our perception of reality is only just beginning, and it will continue to evolve in ways that challenge and redefine the boundaries of creativity, media, and society itself.

Conclusion

As we reflect on the journey of **Sora** and its place within the rapidly evolving landscape of AI-driven video creation, we are reminded of both the immense potential and the challenges that come with such powerful tools. From its humble beginnings as a limited-access platform to its current status as a game-changer in the world of video production, Sora has emerged as a beacon of innovation. Its capabilities, ranging from generating lifelike visuals to producing abstract and surreal animations, have already begun to reshape how we think about content creation. But while its features are revolutionary, they come with limitations that need to be considered carefully.

On one hand, Sora allows creators to break free from the traditional constraints of video production. Its ability to generate videos with a wide array of visual styles and themes means that artists, marketers, and storytellers can experiment and produce content that was once reserved for professionals with access to expensive equipment and software. The interface is intuitive, and the prompt-driven video generation process allows users to interact with the system in a way that feels almost like co-creating with an intelligent collaborator. It offers a rich set of features, from customized scene transitions to text integration and the ability to remix existing content. These features make it a powerful tool for creators, providing a new level of creative freedom and efficiency.

Yet, as with all cutting-edge technologies, there are still limitations that need to be acknowledged. The struggles with object permanence, unrealistic physics, and the inconsistencies that come with photorealism remain significant hurdles. These imperfections are a reminder that while AI is making leaps in video generation, it is not yet flawless. The challenge of creating completely realistic human-like videos, for instance, is still a distant goal, and Sora's ability to navigate the fine line between creativity and realism remains an area of improvement. However, the rapid pace at which AI is advancing suggests that many of these issues may be resolved in the coming years.

Looking ahead, the potential for **Sora** and AI-driven video creation tools is immense. As accessibility to such tools grows, it will open up entirely new possibilities for content creators across industries. The ability to produce high-quality, customized videos at scale will become a standard practice, whether for social media campaigns, advertisements, educational content, or entertainment. This democratization of content creation will likely lead to a surge in innovation and creativity, as more people from diverse backgrounds will be able to contribute their voices and ideas to the global conversation. But with this increased access comes responsibility.

AI tools like Sora should be used with a sense of ethical consideration and foresight. While the technology is exciting, it also carries the potential for misuse, from spreading misinformation to infringing on intellectual property. Responsible usage, including adherence to ethical guidelines and respect for intellectual property, will be key to ensuring that these tools are harnessed for good rather than harm. The conversation around the ethics of AI-generated content, such as the need for watermarking and transparency, is one that will continue to evolve as the technology becomes more ubiquitous.

Ultimately, **Sora** represents a snapshot of the future of video creation—a future where boundaries between human creativity and machine-driven processes blur, offering new opportunities while challenging old notions of what is real, authentic, and possible. The impact of this technology on media and society will only deepen as AI continues to advance. It will reshape industries, redefine how we communicate, and change the way we experience and interact with the media we consume. The potential for creativity, innovation, and expression is limitless, but as we stand on the precipice of this new era, we must remain mindful of the ethical and societal implications. The future of AI-powered video tools like Sora is bright, and it holds the promise of unlocking a new world of creative possibilities—if we wield them with responsibility and foresight.

www.ingramcontent.com/pod-product-compliance
Lightning Source LLC
LaVergne TN
LVHW051705050326
832903LV00032B/4024